AMERICA'S POLITICAL DYSFUNCTION:
A FEW THOUGHTS

AMERICA'S POLITICAL DYSFUNCTION: A FEW THOUGHTS

MITCHELL W. HEDSTROM

AMERICA'S POLITICAL DYSFUNCTION:
A FEW THOUGHTS

iUniverse books may be ordered through booksellers or by contacting:

iUniverse
1663 Liberty Drive
Bloomington, IN 47403
www.iuniverse.com
844-349-9409

Because of the dynamic nature of the Internet, any web addresses or links contained in this book may have changed since publication and may no longer be valid. The views expressed in this work are solely those of the author and do not necessarily reflect the views of the publisher, and the publisher hereby disclaims any responsibility for them.

Any people depicted in stock imagery provided by Getty Images are models, and such images are being used for illustrative purposes only. Certain stock imagery © Getty Images.

ISBN: 978-1-6632-2741-6 (sc)
ISBN: 978-1-6632-2742-3 (e)

Library of Congress Control Number: 2021916606

Print information available on the last page.

iUniverse rev. date: 12/30/2021

CONTENTS

Other book by Author

*Five Generations of Hedstroms: An American
Branch of A Swedish Family*

For Lulu
And with special thanks to Tim

PREFACE

Today, America enjoys a position of being the predominant global power, not only economically and militarily but also politically. However, when considering the next 100 years, there are several reasonably serious threats to this position, some international and others domestic. This book will focus on the latter category.

A general consensus that has developed both in the United States and across the globe is that there is a significant level of dysfunction in America's national politics.[1] The three most-frequently mentioned causes of this dysfunction are the influence of money, lobbyists, and special interests; the management of our government's finances; and the process we use to redraw our Congressional Districts every ten years.

This book will look at each of these three problems, reaching the conclusion that only by amending the U.S. Constitution can we hope to permanently "solve" these three causes of our political dysfunction.

Greenwich, CT
December 20, 2021

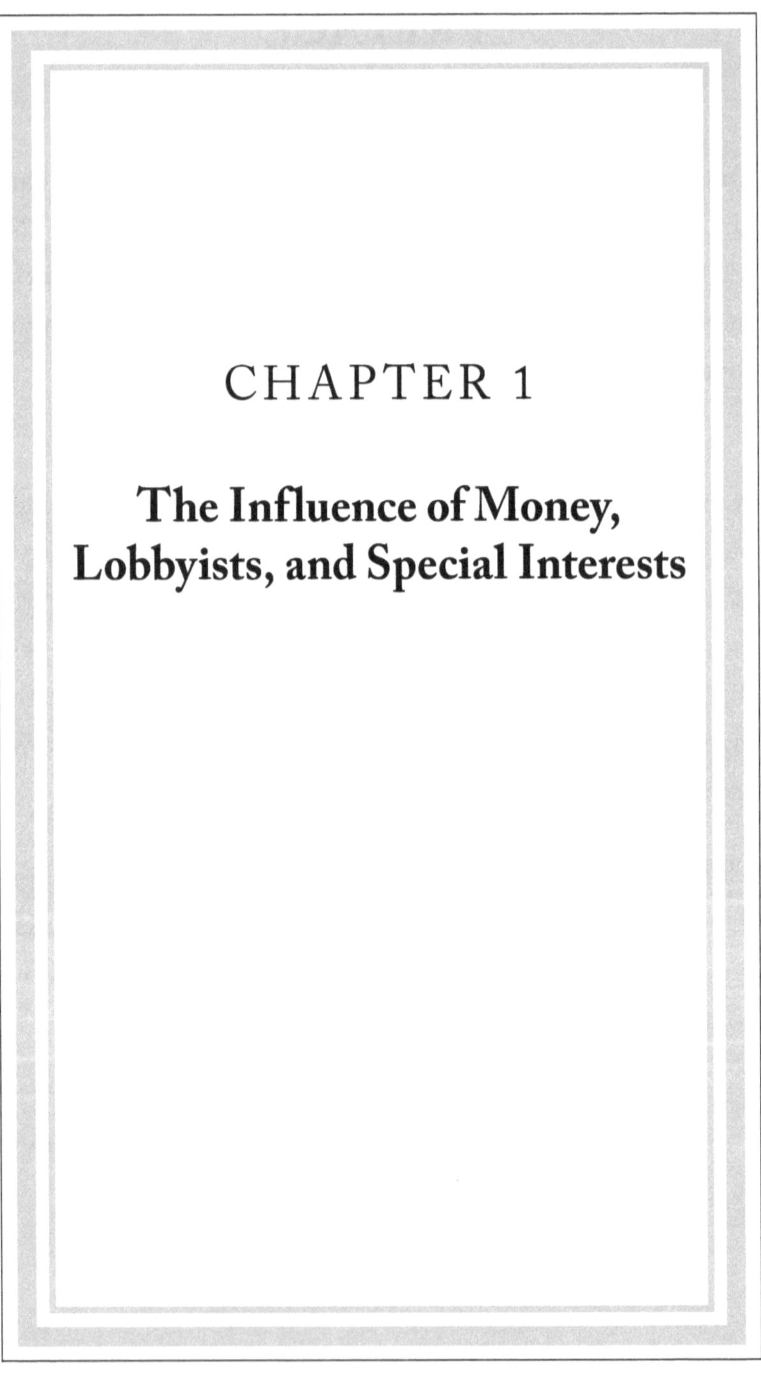

CHAPTER 1

The Influence of Money, Lobbyists, and Special Interests

The first cause of America's political dysfunction to be addressed here is probably the most serious, and in some ways, the most challenging to solve. The main reason it is so challenging is that all of the laws that have been passed to date to either regulate or put caps on the amount of money members of Congress can raise from donations or the amount they can spend on their election campaigns have been struck down by the U.S. Supreme Court as being unconstitutional because they contravene the First Amendment's protection of free speech. It is time to take a fresh look at how the impact of the largest cause of our dysfunction might be lessened.

Background

Members of Congress have developed a huge dependency on raising ever-increasing amounts of money to fund their re-election campaigns. The suppliers of that money – mostly corporations and special interest groups – enjoy their ability to influence the legislative and regulatory processes and the priorities in the federal budgets. The result is what the American Bar Association has referred to as a "mutually reinforcing cycle of dependency."[2]

Donors and special interest groups cannot directly "buy" the vote of a member of Congress as this has been considered "bribery" since 1853, when Congress passed "An Act to Prevent Frauds…"[3] However, they can influence how members of Congress vote on legislation, regulatory decisions, and budgets by making substantial campaign contributions (as long as these contributions are not directly buying the members' votes). Nowadays, much of Washington, D. C. operates in this gray zone, which often involves buying influence.

Members of Congress are generally not venal people; rather, it is the institutions that have become corrupt. Neither side has any interest in stopping the mutual dependency; Congress doesn't want to cut off its access to funding for re-election campaigns and potentially lucrative jobs at lobbying firms when members leave Congress, while the wealthy, the lobbyists, and special interest groups do not wish to relinquish their ability to influence the members of Congress.

There are at least four ways in which wealthy individuals, corporations, lobbyists, and special interest groups cause our political dysfunction. First, as Lawrence Lessig explained in his book *Republic, Lost*, they distort our democracy because our members of Congress must now worry about keeping both their voters and their donors happy to stay in office. Consequently, donors bend and distort our democracy away from dependence on voters and toward a dependence on both voters and donors.

Second, they weaken the trust that Americans have in their Members of Congress. For example, a Gallup Poll conducted in September 2015 found that "majorities believe that most members of Congress are out of touch with average Americans

(79%), are focused on the needs of special interests rather than the needs of their constituents (69%), and corrupt (52%)."[4]

Third, they have a significant influence on the configuration of our tax code. This is largely because wealthier individuals and corporations tend to make most of the campaign contributions; most lower income people do not make campaign contributions. There is little doubt that this has contributed to the increasing levels of income and wealth inequality in the U.S.—a trend that is unsustainable.

Fourth, since members of Congress are required to have their votes on most legislative matters recorded, the big money donors and special interest groups who disagree with the way the members vote can attempt to "take out" those members by organizing traditional media and social media campaigns against them or by getting their membership to organize a grassroots campaign against them in their home districts or states.

Stanford professor Dr. Francis Fukuyama, when speaking at the Council on Foreign Relations in September 2015, discussed the problem of extremely well-funded and well-organized interest groups.[5] Under democratic theory, he said, referring to James Madison and Federalist 10, these groups or "factions" should be balancing each other. However, he also stated that "the rise of pretty unconstrained and pretty powerful interest groups means that these groups no longer balance each other out." He described how these groups collectively interact with the polarization in the federal government and the unique system of checks and balances in our highly decentralized system of government, with the result today being that "the U.S. Congress is unrepresentative of the broader interest of the American people because of the role of money in politics." [5]

When a member of Congress runs for office, they realize it takes a lot of money to get elected. A successful run for the House of Representatives can take more than a million dollars, while a successful run for the Senate can take more than ten million dollars. The majority of the money that is raised is spent on purchasing advertising, with the rest mostly spent on staff, administrative needs, and travel expenses.

Once a member of Congress is elected, he or she is given a specific fundraising goal known as "party dues," which are levied by their party leadership to help finance candidates' future campaigns. These dues partly depend on the member's committee assignments because some give members greater access to fundraising than others. Dues are paid to the National Democratic or Republican Congressional Committee; for example, the "National Republican Senatorial Committee" or the "Democratic Congressional Campaign Committee."

These committees help elect members to each house of Congress for each major political party. However, the large amount of money controlled by the party's leadership in each house of Congress can be used as leverage to enforce party discipline when it comes time for voting. Hence, the influence of money is also a cause of the polarization we now see in Congress, where the two major political parties diametrically oppose each other on various topics.

The amount of influence that our country's wealthiest individuals, lobbyists, and special interests exert on our federal government has increased substantially during the last 50 years. Today, it is just the way that modern Washington, D. C. operates—it's part of the culture of the city.

Historical Attempts at Solutions

Let's review the history of the efforts of the U.S. Congress to address this problem. There are two aspects that need to be addressed: the process of regulating the role of lobbyists, whose clients are mostly corporations, and the Supreme Court rulings regarding the constitutionality of putting limits on campaign donations and expenditures.

In the last 75 years, three major pieces of legislation have been enacted into law that are directly related to the role of lobbyists influencing our political process: the Federal Regulation of Lobbying Act (FRLA) of 1946, the Lobbying Disclosure Act (LDA) of 1995, and the Honest Leadership and Open Government Act (HLOGA) of 2007. However, there is a consensus that Congress deliberately designed these pieces of legislation to be relatively ineffective in order to serve their own interests. For example, in 2014, it was found that:

> "The impetus for reform [the LDA of 1995] came from a 1991 study by the GAO that revealed how porous the 1946 Act had become. The study found that 10,000 lobbyists listed in an industry guidebook had failed to register as lobbyists. Of those who had, as many as 94 percent failed to complete their registration forms as required by law."[6]

Then Congress passed the HLOGA of 2007, partly as a reaction to the sentencing of lobbyist Jack Abramhoff in January 2006. However, as reported in a 2016 *Politico* article titled "The Lobbying Reform that Enriched Congress":

> "The [HLOGA] was to be a critical part of restoring the people's trust by reforming ethics and lobbying rules. Instead, it made things worse. Nine years later, the result of the law is very nearly the opposite of what the American public was told it was getting at the time. Not only did the lobbying reform bill fail to slow the revolving door, it created an entire class of professional influencers who operate in the shadows, out of the public eye and unaccountable."

After emerging from prison, Jack Abramhoff stated on CBS' 60 Minutes, "The system hasn't been cleaned up at all. There is arrogance on the part of lobbyists… that no matter what they come up with, we're smarter than they are and we'll overcome it."[7]

The second problem with historical attempts to legislate a solution to this problem is related to a set of U.S. Supreme Court decisions. In 1974, Congress attempted to regulate campaign spending and fundraising when they passed the Federal Election Commission (FEC) Act of 1971, and then proceeded to place legal limits on campaign contributions and expenditures when they amended it in 1974. However, in Buckley v. Valeo in 1976, the U.S. Supreme Court ruled that the limits on election spending in this Act contravened the First Amendment's provision on freedom of speech.

This Supreme Court decision was then followed by two related cases. In First National City Bank v. Bellotti in 1978 and Citizens United v. FEC in 2010, the Court handed down similar decisions. In the latter case, also citing the First Amendment's free speech clause, the Court held that the government could not restrict independent expenditures for political communications by corporations, including non-profits, labor unions, and associations. Finally, in McCutcheon v. FEC in 2014, the Supreme Court decided that aggregate limits on political giving by an individual were unconstitutional. As a result of these Court decisions, there has been a flood of money into our national politics over the last few years.

Most observers have concluded that any attempts by Congress to pass a law that would restrict campaign donations and expenditures would be found unconstitutional. Many refer to this as the "Citizens United Problem."

A Potential Solution

There is a possible 28th amendment to the U.S. Constitution that is now working its way through Congress. It was drafted to fix the aforementioned "Citizens United Problem."

Gallup polled the American public on this topic in January 2010, shortly after oral arguments were heard in the Citizens United case.[8] They found that 57% of Americans consider campaign donations to be a protected form of free speech, while 55% said corporate and union donations should be treated that same way under the law as donations from individuals are treated. So by a small margin, Americans supported the U.S. Supreme Court's Citizens United decision. Then, in a June 2013 poll, Gallup found that 79% of Americans would vote for a law that would put a limit on the amount of money candidates for Congress could raise and spend on their political campaigns. Interestingly, this included 82% of Democrats and 78% of Republicans polled, so the support for such limits is both broad and bi-partisan.

If the Constitution were to be amended so that Congress was allowed to set limits on how much candidates could raise and limits on how much they could spend for any national office (i.e., the presidency, the Senate and the House), the question then arises as to what might be the scope and wording of such an amendment. Fortunately, much of the work on this topic has been done by an organization called "American Promise." Their website is: https://americanpromise.net. The stated goal of this organization is to solve the "Citizens United Problem" with an amendment to the constitution.

In 2019, Congressmen Theodore Deutch (D-FL), James McGovern (D-MA), Jamie Raskin (D-MD) and John Katko (R-NY) submitted a joint resolution (HJ Res. #2) to the U.S. House of Representatives that proposes a constitutional amendment saying that "Congress and the states may regulate and set reasonable limits on the raising and spending of money by candidates and others to influence elections." This resolution now has 220 of the 290 supporters in the House needed to reach the two-thirds threshold for approving such resolutions in that chamber.

In the U.S. Senate, Thomas Udall (D-NM), along with many other Senators, submitted a similar joint resolution (SJ Res. #19) that now has 51 Senators supporting it. The U.S. constitution requires 67 Senators or two-thirds to support it in order to reach the required threshold in that chamber. This resolution has bipartisan support in the Senate.[9]

The American People Want a Solution

As frustration builds within the country, the elected leaders are now beginning to feel the pressure to address this problem. For example, in our 2020 presidential election, several Democratic candidates echoed the theme of the influence of big money and special interests. Bernie Sanders said that "real change always takes place from the bottom up and not from the top down," while he also proposed "an agenda that works for every man, woman, and child in the country rather than the corporate elite and the 1%." Similarly, Elizabeth Warren said that she wants "to build an America that won't just work for those at the top but that will work for everyone." Finally, Tom Steyer said that "corporations have bought our government and we need to return power to the people."

While this theme, as mentioned by these three candidates, resonates with Americans who feel that our government has been rigged in favor of the wealthy and the corporations, the political rhetoric will not satisfy the American voters. They need a vision for how we can rectify the current situation.

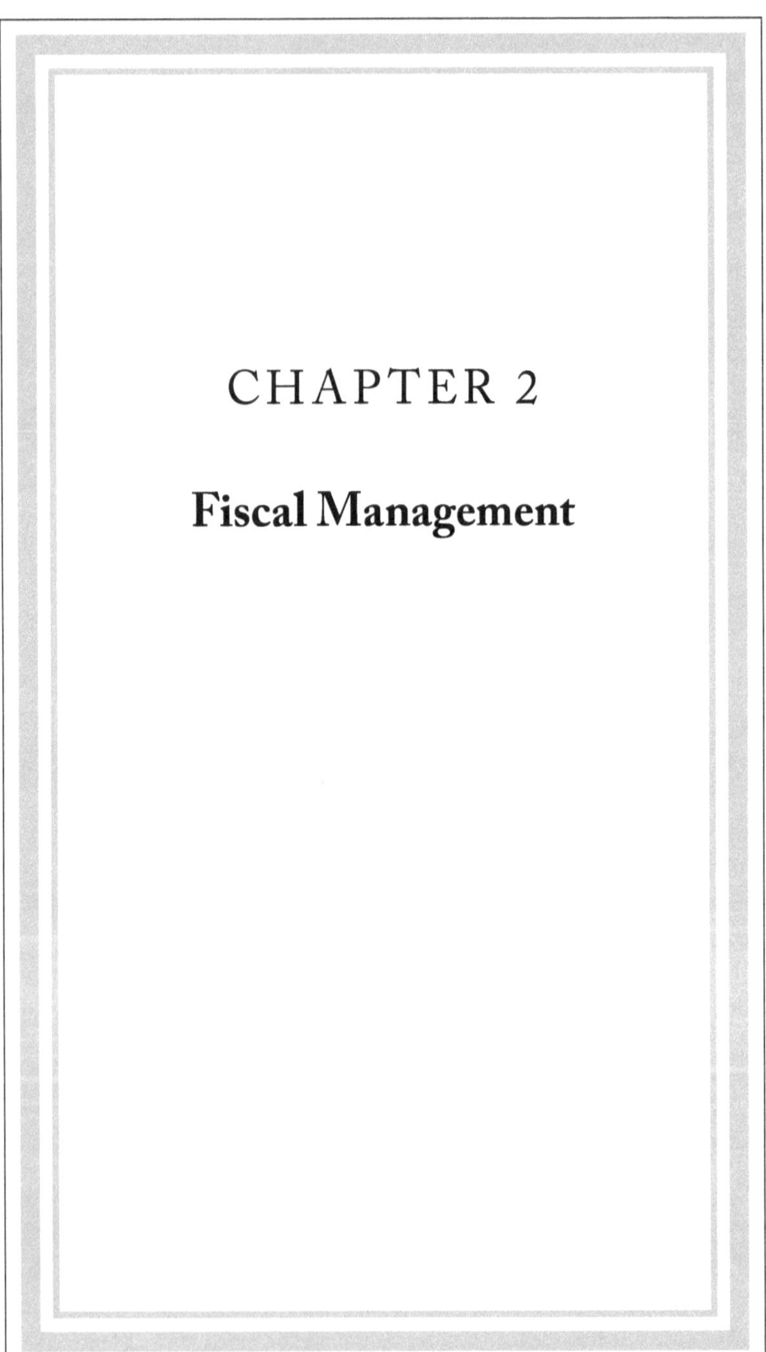

CHAPTER 2

Fiscal Management

Any major country threatening to default on its debt obligations, or one that closes down its federal government for more than one month as a tactic in budget negotiations, is not operating at a level that inspires great confidence and respect. The American people deserve to have a better process for managing their country's finances.

Americans currently assign a low priority to their country's debt and deficits. In the recent low interest rate environment, they have placed a much higher priority on other topics. Meanwhile, the rest of the world has grown increasingly alarmed that America's irresponsible fiscal management could trigger a rapid decline in the relative value of the U.S. dollar.

The Federal Reserve Bank of St. Louis reports that the value of the U.S. dollar relative to an ounce of gold has declined by 25.6% over the last five years ending June 30, 2021.[10] Actually, there is often some confusion regarding the price of gold, as when the "price" of gold goes up, it is really the value of the currency (e.g., the U.S. dollar) that is going down relative to a fixed amount of gold, such as an ounce. As the U.S. dollar declines, it takes more U.S. dollars to purchase the same ounce of gold. For example, if the price of gold in U.S. dollars were to go from $1,000 per ounce to $2,000 per ounce, it is really the value of the U.S. dollar that has declined by 50%.

There is an often-overlooked creative safeguard for Americans who are concerned about the state of their federal government's finances. This safeguard comprises a Constitutional amendment to permit Americans to hold gold and silver and to be able to buy and sell them without incurring any tax liability.

Background

Unfortunately, American voters continue to want much more federal government than they are willing to pay for in taxes. The two major political parties have argued and debated over the appropriate levels of taxes and spending in a seemingly endless tug-of-war for decades. All of the legislative solutions that have been tried over this period have failed to arrest the downward trajectory in the overall quality of the federal government's finances. One of the more recent bi-partisan attempts to get better control of the fiscal deficits was the National Commission on Fiscal Responsibility and Reform, also known as the Simpson-Bowles Commission. It failed to get the super-majority of 14 votes among the 18 Commission members that were required under the executive order that created the Commission in order for its recommendations to go to the full Congress for approval or rejection.

As of March 31, 2021, the total federal debt held by the public was $22 trillion, up from $9.7 trillion ten years earlier.[11] This is the amount of debt that the federal government borrows in the financial markets by issuing treasury securities. According to the St. Louis Federal Reserve, the level of this debt, as a percentage of GDP, was approximately 99.8% on March 31, 2021, up from about 63.2% ten years earlier.[12] As the IMF recently stated, "The U.S. public debt is on an unsustainable path and policy adjustments are needed to lower the fiscal deficit and put public debt on a gradual downward path over the medium term."[13]

Meanwhile, the Congressional Budget Office estimates that the federal budget deficit for the fiscal year ending September 30, 2021, will be $3.0 trillion.[14]

In July 2019, a Gallup poll asked Americans, "What do you think is the most important problem facing the country today?"[15] The fiscal deficit and debt were not even among the top 11 issues that were mentioned—issues mentioned by at least 3% of the respondents. So solving this problem is not in vogue at the present time. However, given the clearly unsustainable trends, it is only a matter of time before this issue moves back up the voters' list of national priorities. In the meantime, there are ultimately two checks on the level of fiscal deficits and federal debts: pressure from the voters and pressure from the financial markets. Both of these sources of potential pressure remain quite subdued at the present time.

In fact, in 2020, some of the Democratic candidates for President campaigned to provide "Medicare for All" and "Free College Tuition." Also lingering in the background is a belief among some in Modern Monetary Theory (MMT) as an alternative to mainstream macroeconomic theory. MMT essentially argues that governments should create new money by using fiscal policy.

Viewed from the broadest possible perspective, the United States enjoys a position regarding its federal government finances that is relatively better than almost any other country. In addition to having the world's largest economy, it also has the world's reserve currency. Almost all of the debt of the U.S. that is held by the public is denominated in U. S dollars. This means that the U.S. government controls the printing presses that print U.S. dollars that it uses to repay its own debt. This gives the country an enormous advantage relative to other countries.

According to the IMF, during the fourth quarter of 2020, approximately 59% of the international reserves held by countries all over the world were denominated in U.S. dollars—the lowest level in 25 years.[16] The U.S. currently enjoys an "AA+" credit rating by Standard & Poor's (S&P), meaning that there are only ten other countries in the world with a similar or higher sovereign credit rating, out of more than 100 countries rated by S&P.[17]

A Worst-Case Scenario

The reason people want to protect themselves from a rapid decline in the U.S. dollar is that they want to hedge their investments from losing value on their U.S. dollar holdings. Some worry about a worst-case scenario where the U.S. dollar declines precipitously.

What would a worst-case scenario look like? If a country has almost no reserves, hyperinflation, and very little access to any additional credit, it can be presumed to be essentially bankrupt. However, eventually, such countries can work with international financial institutions such as the IMF and the World Bank to get help recovering from their dire situation. To illustrate this point, countries in this type of situation include Germany in the early 1920s, when a loaf of bread cost 200 billion marks, and Zimbabwe during the period of 2008 to 2009, when its month-on-month inflation rate was about 80 billion percent per month.[18]

Some would argue that the U.S. is a different type of country since it possesses the world's reserve currency. However, this doesn't mean that many investors no longer worry about a worst-case scenario for the U.S. It just means that the U.S. would take longer to suffer serious consequences than other countries in a similar situation but without the reserve currency status.

If the U.S. continues to slide toward a much worse fiscal situation, several key indicators will begin to flash. For example, the financial markets will begin to indicate signs of trouble with a weakened U.S. dollar, as measured by the trade-weighted index, higher interest rates being demanded by bondholders for holding U.S. Treasury obligations, a higher level of inflation, and a lower level of international currency reserves being held in U.S. dollars. An indicator for the American voters would be that they see the debt and deficits as a much higher priority on their worry list in public opinion polls.

Americans who worry about the worsening state of their country's finances would normally be able to protect themselves by putting some of their savings in gold and silver. However, although Americans are now able to enjoy the ability to invest in gold and silver, this hasn't always been the case. History has shown that in times of great stress, this option can be taken away. For example, in April 1933, President Franklin D. Roosevelt issued an executive order forbidding the hoarding of gold coins, gold bullion, and gold certificates within the continental United States. Then, in 1934, Congress passed the Gold Reserve Act that prohibited the private ownership of gold in the United States.[19]

The limitation on gold ownership in the United States was repealed after President Gerald Ford signed a bill legalizing private ownership of gold coins, bars, and certificates by an act of Congress that went into effect in December 1974.[20] However, Americans who worry about their government's deteriorating finances will always have the fear that the federal government could once again confiscate their gold.

A Possible Solution

An amendment to the U.S. Constitution that would permit Americans to hold gold or silver coins, bars, and certificates without restrictions would be one possible safeguard for Americans worried about their federal government's deteriorating finances. Such an amendment could also state that Americans could purchase and sell such gold or silver without incurring any tax liability. The reason for the latter provision about taxes is that today, if an American were to sell their holdings of gold or silver, any gain on their investment in such metals could be subject to taxation. Consequently, someone with a large hedged investment in gold or silver at the time of a spike in the metal's prices could face a large tax bill once their investment was monetized.

The impact of such an amendment on the federal government would be subtle. At first, there would be almost no visible impact, provided the U.S. government's finances remained relatively stable. For example, during the last few calendar years, American investors would have obtained a higher return by investing in the S&P 500 index than by investing in gold.

The practical implication of such an amendment for individual Americans would be that it would offer them permanent protection from the risk that their holdings of gold and silver could be confiscated in the future or that any gains on the sale of such holdings could be taxed. If the fiscal position of the U.S. continues to deteriorate and the level of the federal debt continues to increase, then such an amendment would make it more likely that Americans would invest a larger portion of their savings in gold and silver in order to protect themselves.

CHAPTER 3

The Process of Redrawing Congressional Districts

America is currently a divided country. Contentious issues such as abortion, gun control, immigration, and establishing the appropriate level of taxes and spending have all caused deep tensions among its citizens. In fact, our elected leaders are even more polarized than the people they represent. Why is this?

One significant cause can be traced back to the process that our states use to redraw the borders of their congressional districts once the U.S. census is completed every ten years. In most states, the political parties controlling the state legislatures now use sophisticated computer software to design districts that are either very Republican or very Democratic. The result is that our elected leaders in the House of Representatives are now much more worried about their future primary elections than they are about a general election, so they move more to the right or the left on issues than the position of many of their constituents.

Although reform efforts have led several states to adopt independent non-partisan or bi-partisan redistricting commissions, it is time to consider a constitutional amendment to establish one clear standard for how all 50 states design their congressional districts.

Background

In July 2020, a Gallup poll found that only 18% of American voters "approve of the way Congress is handling its job."

However, during three recent elections, the percentages of re-elected members of the House of Representatives were: 95.4% in 2014, 96.7% in 2016, and 91% in 2018, according to the Center for Responsive Politics. Many people have asked why the American voters don't fire the members of Congress if they are doing such a poor job, instead of re-electing them. Although money and name recognition play a role, the truth is that we have a political system that is rigged to favor incumbents, and the American people don't like it.

Perhaps the most important starting point for any discussion about congressional re-districting is the language in the U.S. Constitution. Article 1, Section 2 reads, "The House of Representatives shall be comprised of Members chosen every second year by the people of the several states..." In 1913, the 17th amendment established the popular election of U.S. Senators by the people of the states. Prior to that, U.S. Senators had been elected by their state legislatures.

The term *gerrymander* dates back to 1812 when the Governor of Massachusetts, Elbridge Gerry, signed a bill that created a district that apparently looked like a salamander. The Reapportionment Act of 1929 withdrew the size and population requirements for congressional districts that had been previously stated in the Apportionment Act of 1911 and set the number of total House seats at 435. Since each state must have at least one district, there are now seven states that have only one congressional district. The prior apportionment acts had required that districts be contiguous, compact, and equally populated. However, the process of gerrymandering enables the political party that controls the state legislature to deliberately manipulate the district boundaries for partisan political advantage.

There are a series of decisions by the U.S. Supreme Court that provide some legal clarity to the states on the topic of redistricting. They can be summarized as follows: the Court established the famous "one person, one vote" principle as a standard for legislative redistricting (Gray v. Sanders). They then decided that House districts must be approximately equal in population (Wesberry v. Sanders) and held that gerrymandering a House district based on racial or ethnic criteria is unconstitutional. Although they found that a particular case involving extreme partisan gerrymandering was unconstitutional and did not agree on how this could be defined (Gill v. Whitford), they upheld the right of voters in one state to remove the authority to redraw districts from the state legislature and vest it in an independent redistricting commission (Arizona State Legislature v. Arizona Independent Redistricting Commission). Finally, in 2019, the Court ruled that while partisan gerrymandering may be "incompatible with democratic principles," the federal courts cannot review such allegations as they present "nonjusticiable political questions outside of the remit of these courts" (Rucho v. Common Cause).

Independent Redistricting Commissions

Since the U.S. Supreme Court's decision involving the Arizona State Legislature in 2015, approximately 17 states have established some type of independent redistricting commission.[21] These commissions generally fall into three categories: those that have the primary responsibility for drawing congressional district boundaries; those that act in an advisory capacity, where they may assist the state legislature with drawing the district lines; and those that have a backup role, where they will make the decision regarding congressional district boundaries if the legislature is unable to agree.

Former California governor Arnold Schwarzenegger established an institute bearing his name at USC, and one of its goals has been to provide assistance to states that would like to set up an independent redistricting commission. It should also be noted that California has adopted a "modified open primary" approach to congressional elections, where the top two vote-getters go on to the general election, regardless of their party affiliation. The effect of this approach is to allow for more competition in heavily partisan districts.

The Hamilton, Cohen & Frye Proposal

In July 2020, three distinguished Americans authored an article that was published in *The Washington Post* ("How Congress Can Stop Gerrymandering").[22] These three individuals were

Lee Hamilton, Former Democratic Representative of Indiana and former Vice Chairman of the 9/11 Commission; William Cohen, former Republican U.S. Senator from Maine and former Secretary of Defense; and Alton Frye, former President of the Council on Foreign Relations.

Hamilton, Cohen, and Frye's article began by quoting Justice John Roberts' opinion in the U.S. Supreme Court's Rucho case, where he said that drawing districts to assure a party's advantage was "incompatible with democratic values." They then went on note that Article 1 – Section 5 of the U.S. Constitution gives the House the power to act on their own to design a process to accept or reject Members that fail to meet the qualifications they establish for service. The specific language says that "each House shall be the judge of the elections, returns, and qualifications of its own Members." They point out that such action by the House would not require any involvement by the U.S. Senate or by the Executive Branch.

Before making their recommendation, Hamilton, Cohen, and Frye explained that "in the republic's carly decades, congressional delegations were elected on a statewide basis… only after 1842 did Congress require states to conduct elections of single members in defined districts." [22] In the article, they also said, "At the core of Roberts' opinion is the concern that the courts have no workable standard to judge how much divergence between statewide and district-level party votes is too much." Their recommendation was that "there needs to be a mechanism [for the House] to assess districts and whether those who designed them intended to distort the will of the statewide constituency... It could, for example, establish an independent advisory body to analyze state redistricting plans and report on any that embody intentional, excessive partisan exploitation."

In a separate article in the *PA Times* (a publication of the American Society for Public Administration) in January 2019, Alton Frye argued that with extreme gerrymandering, the "state legislatures have usurped the power vested by the Constitution in the 'people of the states.'"[23] His recommendation was "to allocate the number of House seats in each state according to the percentage of each party's vote for House seats on a statewide basis... A straightforward process could mesh the statewide electoral outcome with the results in each district. Take a hypothetical state with ten congressional districts. Imagine that party A wins a statewide total of 60 percent of the votes cast for the House and party B attracts 40 percent. Those results would entitle party A to six of the state's ten congressional seats, with party B earning four seats." [23]

A Proposed Constitutional Amendment

It seems clear that the 50 states are not all likely to establish independent redistricting commissions with a uniform approach that eliminates extreme partisan gerrymandering anytime soon. It also seems clear that while the U.S. Supreme Court recognizes that such gerrymandering is "incompatible with democratic values," [22] the Court's justices were concerned that there is "no workable standard to judge how much divergence between statewide and district-level party votes is too much." The solution proposed by the three authors of the *Washington Post* article seems interesting; however, for those who doubt Congress' ability to police itself, there is another approach—preparing a constitutional amendment.

The scope and language of such an amendment could re-establish the original intent of the Constitution to have the members of the House chosen by the "people of the several states" and not by state legislatures. As Alton Frye recommended in his *PA Times* article, it could then provide for the allocation of the number of House seats within the state based on the proportion of the total votes cast for each political party in the House races within that state.

Finally, when it comes to designing the boundaries for the congressional districts, states could be required to design their districts based on contiguous towns and cities. To the extent necessary to achieve the required number of people in each district, one town or city could be divided into two along an imaginary north-south line that is as straight as is practical.

The reason for the last aspect of this proposal—the requirement for contiguous towns and cities—is to tie the local politics of towns and cities to the national politics of House districts, which is something that is missing in today's politics.

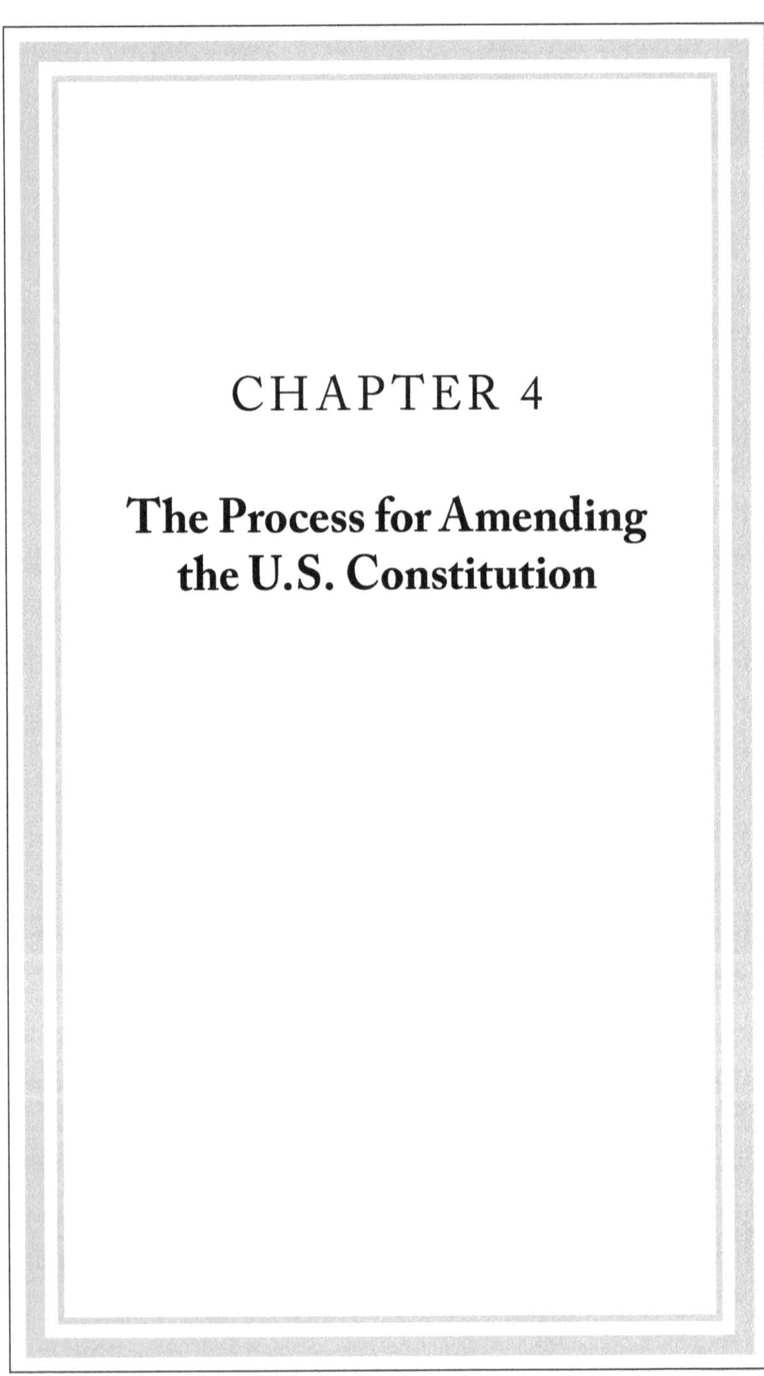

CHAPTER 4

The Process for Amending the U.S. Constitution

The framers provided us with the amendment process in Article V of the Constitution. They knew that there would be circumstances that would require the Constitution to be revised or updated.

Setting aside the ten amendments that comprise the Bill of Rights and the 27th amendment (which took more than 202 years to ratify), we see that a majority of the remaining 16 amendments were ratified within one year of being proposed by Congress. Therefore, although the ratification process will not be easy, it would appear that the real challenge in working to amend the constitution will most likely be to obtain the requisite two-thirds votes from both houses of Congress.

Article V of the Constitution provides two alternatives for proposing an amendment. The first method—getting a resolution passed by two-thirds of both houses of Congress—has been used for all of our current 27 amendments. However, the second method—getting two-thirds of the state legislatures to call for a convention for proposing amendments—was used effectively as a bargaining strategy in the case of the 17th amendment (which required Senators to be elected directly by the voters).

In the case of the 17th amendment, many states began sending Congress applications for conventions. As the number of applications neared the two-thirds bar, Congress finally acted. As Jay Bybee, writing in the *Northwestern University Law Review* in 1997, explained, "By 1910, [there were] 31 state legislatures [that] had passed resolutions calling for a constitutional amendment allowing direct election, and in the same year, ten Republican Senators who were opposed to reform were forced out of their seats, acting as a 'wake-up call' to the Senate."[24] Therefore, in order to avoid the uncertainty of a national constitutional convention, both houses passed the resolution for the 17th amendment.

In order to solve or fix the three problems discussed in the earlier chapters, building a grassroots movement will be a necessary first step. In the case of the first problem or cause of our dysfunction (i.e., money, lobbyists, and special interests), the organization called American Promise, referred to above, has already built a grassroots organization and has made quite good progress. That organization and its president, Jeff Clements, provide a good example of how this can be done.

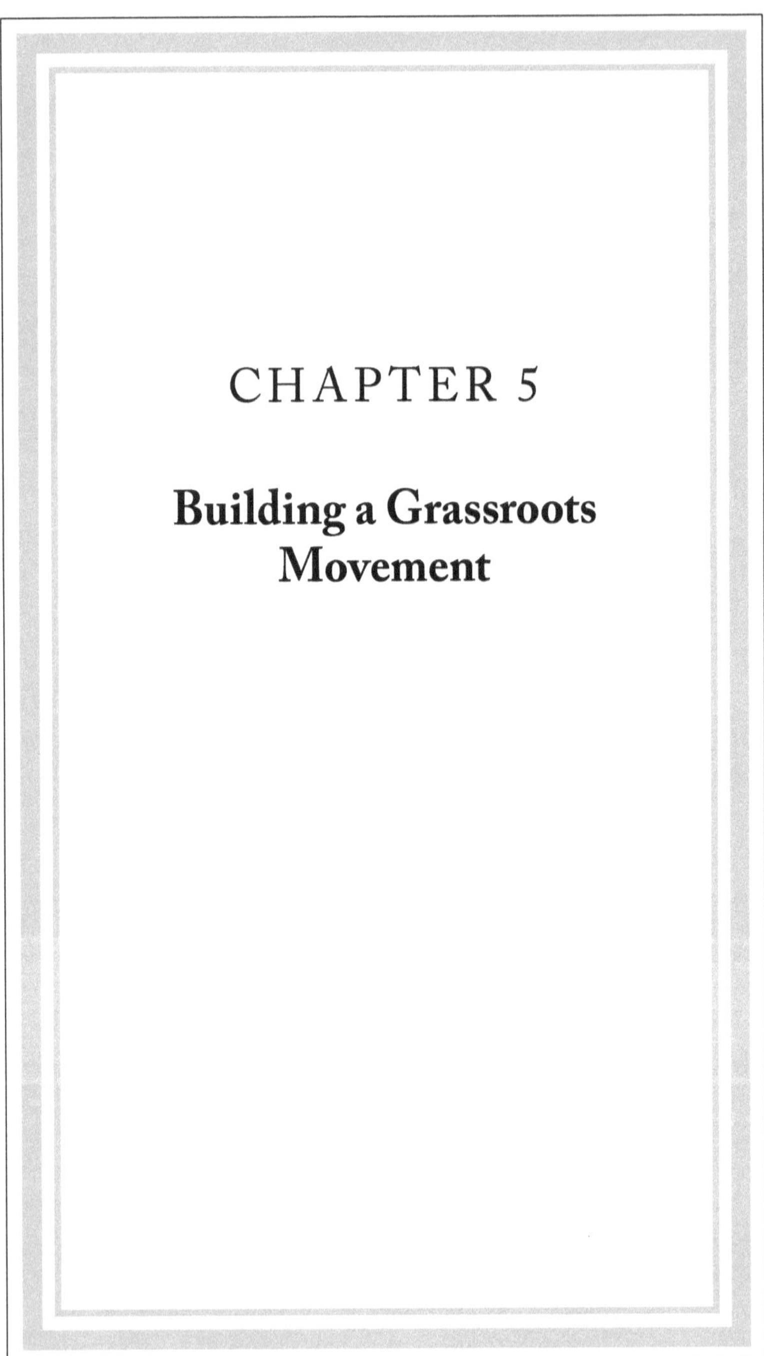

CHAPTER 5

Building a Grassroots Movement

If one's overall objective is to fix a significant portion of America's political dysfunction, it makes sense to focus initial efforts on helping get the pending 28th amendment passed by Congress and ratified by the states as soon as possible. As mentioned above, the organization called American Promise is now leading this effort. However, as members of this group will tell you, this is an incredibly difficult project. Therefore, what follows is a proposal to build a new grassroots organization that can complement the efforts of American Promise.

Before thinking about all 50 states, it makes sense to begin with a small pilot or 'proof of concept.' Such a pilot might consist of six relatively small towns in one state. The initial organizing event could be a debate between the leaders of the two major political parties in each of the pilot towns. The debate could be scheduled a few months before the next election of the town's leaders. In order for this debate to succeed, it will be necessary to engage the local business community for each pilot town. They should be able to help with fundraising and identifying potential donors. Getting agreement on the date and venue will be an important step towards ensuring the debate's success.

For each of the debates, the moderator might be the editor of the local newspaper or magazine to help see that there is a significant level of publicity. Creating a video recording the debate would enable the organizers to put the video on YouTube afterwards. The model for the debate should be the format used by the "Munk Debates" in Canada (https://munkdebates.com). The local branch of the League of Women's Voters should be invited to co-sponsor the debates. The local business community should help with fundraising and identifying potential donors.

Prior to the debate in each town, the organizers should commission a public opinion poll that asks the following two questions of a sample of registered voters in that town: (a) "Do you approve of the job that your elected leaders in the town of ____ are doing?" and (b) "If you could wave a magic wand and change any one thing about the town of ______, what would that be?"

The first question, taken from a similar question asked regularly of our U. S. presidents, is usually referred to as the approval rating question. When it is used for the pilot towns, it will enable the new grassroots organization to rank the towns by their approval ratings. The second question will enable the organizers to identify the top issues of concern to the registered voters in each town. The opinion polls should be conducted prior to the town debate in each pilot town. Once the two major political parties in each town agree to participate in the debate, they should be given access to the raw data from the opinion poll in an appropriate format – something elected leaders will be anxious to have.

There are various possible polling firms that might be considered. If the firms know that this project is being designed to be rolled out across the entire country, they might be interested in reasonable terms for being engaged for the first few polls that comprise the pilot.

After the debates, there are three other ideas that might help to enhance the pilot project:

- A report that can be printed and distributed to all registered voters in each of the pilot towns. The format should be similar to a magazine. The leaders of the two main political parties should be offered one page in the front to write a letter to the voters. It should also provide the voters with a summary of their town's ranking in approval ratings and the top issues of concern to the voters in that town. The local business community can run advertisements.

- Second, a "Hero X" competition might be organized for the pilot towns. Hero X is a crowdsourcing platform for innovators (https://www.herox.com). Like its sister organization "X Prize" that provides competitions for outer space and other large projects that generally have a prize of more than $1 million, Hero X is a smaller scale version of the same concept, with prizes of generally less than $1 million. Hero X is described on its website as being "a modest, democratic alternative to X-Prizes multi-million dollar curated challenges." The Hero X competition for this project might provide a way to get the pilot towns to compete against each other for a prize.

- Third, there is a company called Votizen that is headquartered in Mountain View, CA that has been described as "a consumer technology company that harnesses social networks to create a connected electorate of voters." Its website (https://votizen.com) allows its members, which it calls "Votizens," to learn about issues and elections and take collective action with other committed voters through social media. The firm verifies that each voice belongs to a real voter in the real world. They might be asked to help collaborate on the pilot project.

In summary, these are only a few ideas that have the potential to move the proposed 28th amendment toward ratification. If the pilot project is successful, it can be rolled out to the states where the most help is needed in getting the U. S. Senators and Representatives on board with the proposed amendment. Once the 28th amendment has been ratified, the other two amendments in Chapters Two and Three can be taken on as new projects.

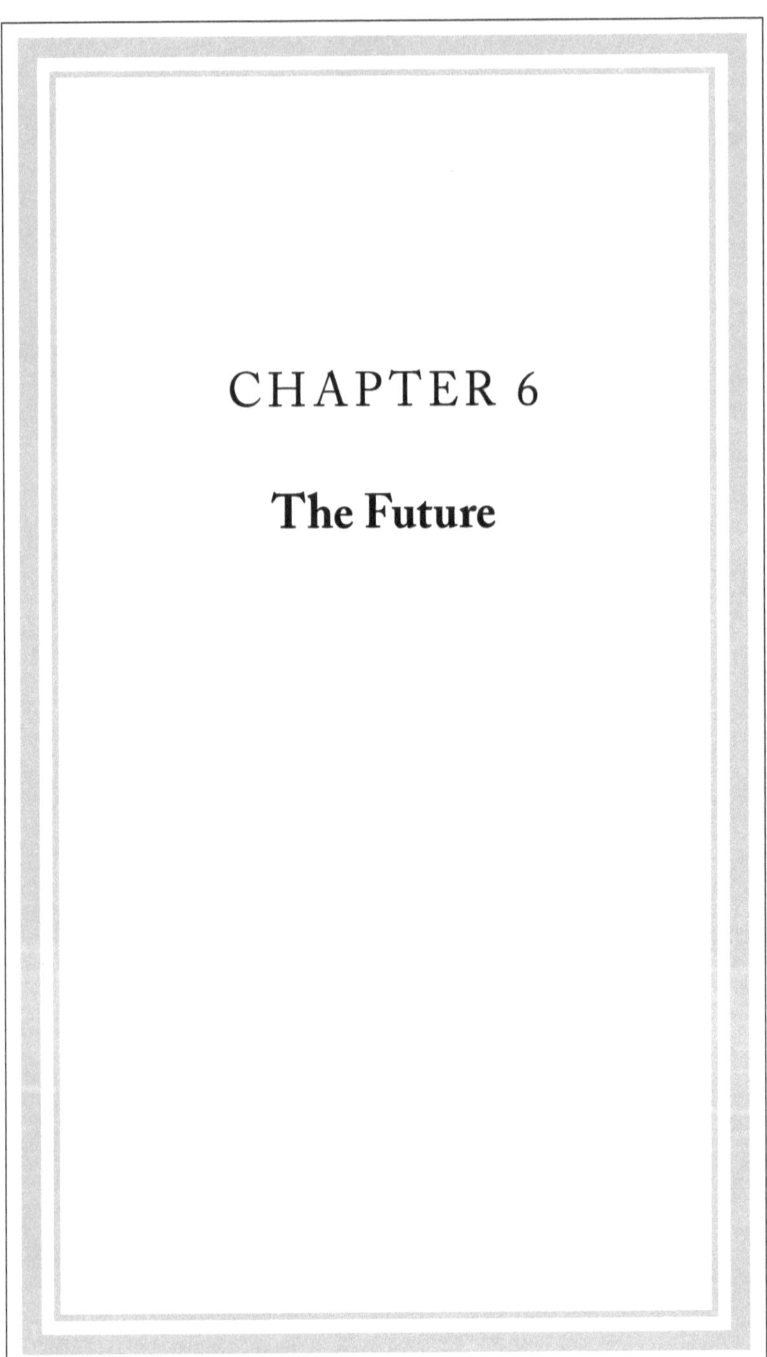

CHAPTER 6

The Future

Perhaps one or more of our elected leaders will support an effort to build a grassroots movement to push for the constitutional amendment to solve the Citizens United problem proposed above. They might remember that one of the many reasons Abe Lincoln was one of our greatest presidents was that he managed to get the 13th amendment (a ban on slavery) passed by both houses of Congress while he was president.

Also, perhaps one or more of our country's wealthy individuals will lend their support to this effort.

Summary

Developing solutions for our political dysfunction—ones that would gain broad bipartisan support—could significantly strengthen our American democracy so that it can be even more of a shining example for the rest of the world as to how a truly successful liberal democracy can work.

American citizens have a huge stake in the future success of the American experiment. Our honor and common sense tell us that we need to do this for our children and our grandchildren. More than one million Americans have died fighting in various wars since our country was founded. It is clear that working for the passage of these proposed constitutional amendments to solve the biggest sources of our political dysfunction is a noble cause worth supporting wholeheartedly.

The cause for American democracy is, in great measure, the cause for mankind, which is what Abe Lincoln referred to in 1862 when he told Congress, "We shall nobly save, or meanly lose, the last best hope of earth."[25] Perhaps the U.S. can increase the extent to which we inspire people in other parts of the world, leading by setting a good example that others can admire. As former New York City Mayor Michael Bloomberg said, "When people vote with their feet, they come here."[26]

NOTES

Preface:

1 Economist, "What's Gone Wrong with Democracy." Essay; March 1, 2014.

Chapter 1:

2 American Bar Assn. "Lobbying Law in the Spotlight." Report on the task force on federal lobbying laws; January 3, 2011.

3 "An Act to Prevent Frauds Upon the Treasury of the United States." February 26, 1853.

4 "Majority of Americans See Congress as Out of Touch, Corrupt." Gallop – Politics; Sept. 28, 2015.

5 Council on Foreign Relations. "A Conversation with Francis Fukuyama." Sept. 15, 2015.

6 The Nation. "Where Have All the Lobbyists Gone?" February 19, 2014.

7 "Inside Capitol Corruption." CBS, 60 Minutes.

8 "Public Agrees with Court: Campaign Money is Free Speech." Gallop – Politics; Jan 22, 2010.

9 Jeff Clements, President, American Promise.

Chapter 2:

10 Federal Reserve Bank of St. Louis. Gold Fixing Price, 10:30am London Time in London Bullion Market, based in USD. Price on 6/29/21 was 1,769.6 and on 6/30/16 it was 1,317.

11 Federal Reserve Bank of St. Louis. Federal Debt Held by the Public.

12 Federal Reserve Bank of St. Louis. Federal Debt Held by the Public as a Percent of Gross Domestic Product.

13 Xinhua. June 7, 2019. "IMF Says U. S. Public Debt is on an Unsustainable Path".

14 Congressional Budget Office. "An Update to the Budget and Economic Outlook: 2021 to 2031." July 2021.

15 Gallop. "Most Important Problem." June 2021.

16 IMF Blog. US Dollar Share of Global Foreign Exchange Reserves Drops to 25 Year Low." May 5, 2021.

17 Countryeconomy.com. "Sovereign Ratings List." July 22, 2021.

18 "On the Measurement of Zimbabwe's Hyperinflation." Cato Journal, Spring/Summer 2009.

19 Federal Reserve History. "Gold Reserve Act of 1934."

20 NY Times. "Bill Signed to Allow Owning Gold in US." August 15, 1974.

Chapter 3:

21 National Conference of State Legislatures; "2009 Redistricting Commission Table"; June 28, 2006.

22 Washington Post. July 17, 2020. "How Congress Can Stop Gerrymandering".

23 PA Times. January 28, 2019. "A Constitutional Standard to End Gerrymandering."

Chapter 4:

24 Bybee, Jay S. "Ulysses at the Mast." Northwestern Univ. School of Law, Vol. 91, No. 2. 1977.

Chapter 6:

AUTHOR'S BIOGRAPHY

The author worked for Citigroup for 30 years, eventually as a Vice President and Member of their Restructuring Committee. He received his Master of Science degree from the Massachusetts Institute of Technology. He is a member of the Council on Foreign Relations and lives with his wife in Greenwich, CT and Warwick, Bermuda. Their daughter currently lives and works in New York City.